D1526712

EXAMINING ISSUES THROUGH
POLITICAL CARTOONS

The Vietnam War

Edited by Louise I. Gerdes

Bruce Glassman, *Vice President*
Bonnie Szumski, *Publisher*
Helen Cothran, *Managing Editor*
Scott Barbour, *Series Editor*

GREENHAVEN PRESS
An imprint of Thomson Gale, a part of The Thomson Corporation

THOMSON
™
GALE

Detroit • New York • San Francisco • San Diego • New Haven, Conn.
Waterville, Maine • London • Munich

LIBRARY OF CONGRESS CATALOGING-IN-PUBLICATION DATA

The Vietnam War / Louise I. Gerdes, book editor.
    p. cm. — (Examining issues through political cartoons)
Includes bibliographical references (p.) and index.
ISBN 0-7377-2531-1 (lib. : alk. paper)
    1. Vietnamese conflict, 1961–1975—Caricatures and cartoons. 2. United States—Politics and government—1961–1969—Caricatures and cartoons. 3. United States—Politics and government—1969–1974—Caricatures and cartoons. I. Gerdes, Louise I., 1953– . II. Series.

DS557.72.V55 2005
959.7043'373'0207—dc22   2004047458

Printed in the United States of America

Contents

Foreword

Political cartoons, also called editorial cartoons, are drawings that do what editorials do with words—express an opinion about a newsworthy event or person. They typically appear in the opinion pages of newspapers, sometimes in support of that day's written editorial, but more often making their own comment on the day's events. Political cartoons first gained widespread popularity in Great Britain and the United States in the 1800s when engravings and other drawings skewering political figures were fashionable in illustrated newspapers and comic magazines. By the beginning of the 1900s, editorial cartoons were an established feature of daily newspapers. Today, they can be found throughout the globe in newspapers, magazines, and online publications and the Internet.

Art Wood, both a cartoonist and a collector of cartoons, writes in his book *Great Cartoonists and Their Art:*

> Day in and day out the cartoonist mirrors history; he reduces complex facts into understandable and artistic terminology. He is a political commentator and at the same time an artist.

The distillation of ideas into images is what makes political cartoons a valuable resource for studying social and historical topics. Editorial cartoons have a point to express. Analyzing them involves determining both what the cartoon's point is and how it was made.

Sometimes, the point made by the cartoon may be one that the reader disagrees with, or considers offensive. Such cartoons expose readers to new ideas and thereby challenge them to analyze and question their own opinions and assumptions. In some extreme cases, cartoons provide vivid examples of the thoughts that lie behind heinous acts; for example, the cartoons created by the Nazis illustrate the anti-Semitism that led to the mass persecution of Jews.

Examining controversial ideas is but one way the study of political cartoons can enhance and develop critical thinking skills. Another aspect to cartoons is that they can use symbols to make their point quickly. For example, in a cartoon in *Euthanasia*, Chuck Asay depicts supporters of a legal "right to die" by assisted suicide as vultures. Vultures are birds that eat dead and dying animals and are often a symbol of repulsive and cowardly predators who take advantage of those who have met misfortune or are vulnerable. The reader can infer that Asay is expressing his opposition to physician-assisted suicide by suggesting that its supporters are just as loathsome as vultures. Asay thus makes his point through a quick symbolic association.

An important part of critical thinking is examining ideas and arguments in their historical context. Political cartoonists (reasonably) assume that the typical reader of a newspaper's editorial page already has a basic knowledge of current issues and newsworthy people. Understanding and appreciating political cartoons often requires such knowledge, as well as a familiarity with common icons and symbolic figures (such as Uncle Sam's representing the United States). The need for contextual information becomes especially apparent in historical cartoons. For example, although most people know who Adolf Hitler is, a lack of familiarity with other German political figures of the 1930s may create difficulty in fully understanding cartoons about Nazi Germany made in that era.

Providing such contextual information is one important way that Greenhaven's Examining Issues Through Political Cartoons series seeks to make this unique and revealing resource conveniently accessible to students. Each volume presents a representative and diverse collection of political cartoons focusing on a particular current or historical topic. An introductory essay provides a general overview of the subject matter. Each cartoon is then presented with accompanying information including facts about the cartoonist and information and commentary on the cartoon itself. Finally, each volume contains additional informational resources, including listings of books, articles, and websites; an index; and (for historical topics) a chronology of events. Taken together, the contents of each anthology constitute an amusing and informative resource for students of historical and social topics.

Introduction

The Vietnam War had such a significant impact on Americans at home that some suggest the Vietnam War was fought on two fronts: in the jungles of Vietnam and in the American conscience. No war since the Civil War had so divided the nation. The breadth of this divide widened over the course of the war. In living rooms nationwide, the American people not only watched a war being waged in Vietnam, but also on university campuses, in city streets, and on the congressional floor. As a result, the American people would begin to question the credibility of their leaders and the role the United States should play in world affairs.

The Casualties of War

The most obvious impacts of the Vietnam War were the loss of American lives and the struggle faced by Vietnam veterans who returned from Vietnam damaged by the war. Although statistics vary, of the more than 2 million Americans who went to Vietnam, more than 58,000 were killed, including 8 nurses. Of that number, 17,539 men left wives behind. Over 300,000 men were wounded; of those, 75,000 were permanently disabled. Approximately 23,000 were 100 percent disabled, and 5,283 lost limbs. Amputation or crippling wounds to the lower extremities were 300 percent higher in Vietnam than in World War II.

In addition to physical disabilities, many who returned from Vietnam bore psychological scars, yet not until the 1980s was anything done to help these veterans adjust. Although most veterans succeeded in making the transition to ordinary civilian life, many did not. More Vietnam veterans committed suicide after the war than had died in it. As many as 750,000 became homeless. Nearly

700,000 draftees had received less than honorable discharges, which prevented their getting education and medical benefits. Although many believed these dysfunctional veterans needed support and medical attention, the Veterans Administration was reluctant to admit the special difficulties they faced and their need for additional benefits until many years later.

The Living Room War

Returning veterans and the families of those who lost their loved ones felt the impact of the war most directly. Those Americans who had not suffered directly nonetheless experienced the horrors of war more intimately than ever before, and this experience changed many people's attitudes toward U.S. involvement in Vietnam. For the first time in history, Americans could see the images of war at home as they watched the evening news in their living rooms. Thus the Vietnam War earned the name "the living room war." These images were so vivid that many viewers were shocked and amazed, and reactions were quite strong. While some believed that the use of the television medium was inappropriate for reporting on the war, others maintained that it gave citizens a new perspective on the nature of war. A large percentage of Americans felt sympathy and gratitude toward American soldiers. Others, however, felt that the war they saw on television was atrocious and unnecessary. One of the more infamous events Americans witnessed on television were the "Zippo raids." American soldiers were filmed as they used their Zippo cigarette lighters to set fire to thatched huts believed to be occupied by Vietcong guerrillas. Reactions to these images caused controversy among American citizens, and some protested.

One of television's most influential newspersons during the war was Walter Cronkite. As the front man for the *CBS Evening News*, Cronkite showed the horrific details of the Vietnam War and provided the latest updates on the war's progress. In the early years of American fighting in Vietnam, most in the media, including Cronkite, supported the government's policies in Vietnam. Because Cronkite was highly trusted by Americans, the general public tended to agree with his position on the war. As the war escalated, however, inconsistencies in government reporting arose. The media were the first to expose these inconsistencies. For example, Lyndon Johnson had led the American people to believe that there was "light at the end of the tunnel" in Vietnam—that the U.S. military was winning the war. However, on January 31, 1968, the North Vietnamese Army and the Vietcong launched the Tet (Vietnamese New Year) Offensive. American combat deaths escalated dramatically, reaching a peak of twelve hundred per month. The Tet Offensive belied government optimism about the war and suggested that the conflict was unwinnable. Cronkite himself spoke out against the claims of politicians and the military, arguing that the war would result in either a stalemate or defeat. President Johnson was said to have remarked to an aide, "Well, if I've lost Cronkite, I've lost middle America." In fact, after the Tet Offensive, more Americans began to oppose the war.

The Pentagon Papers

The print media also had an impact on Americans' attitudes toward the war in Vietnam. In fact, one of the greatest blows to the government's attempts to paint a positive picture of U.S. involvement in Vietnam was the publication of excerpts from a secret three-thousand-page Pentagon study, "History of the U.S. Decision-Making Process on Vietnam Policy," better known as the Pentagon Papers. The *New York Times* obtained a stolen copy of the papers in March 1971 from former Department of Defense official Daniel Ellsberg and began printing a series of excerpts from them on June 13. According to historian Bryan Rommel-Ruiz, "The publication of the Pentagon Papers seriously damaged U.S. involvement in the war. It exposed the secret war in Laos, deficiencies of the military, and the corruption of the South Vietnamese government. . . . Moreover, they revealed how the government deceived the public throughout the 1960s." After the publication of the Pentagon Papers, only 15 percent of Americans supported the war and more than 60 percent thought the war was "immoral." Publication of the Pentagon Papers diminished trust in the government and established a new role for journalism as a government watchdog.

The Antiwar Movement

Those who opposed the war in Vietnam had been working to expose what they believed to be flawed U.S. foreign policy long before the Pentagon Papers were published. The antiwar movement expanded over the course of the Vietnam War, escalating as U.S.

military involvement in Vietnam escalated. As the Vietnam War progressed, the nature of the protests and protesters changed. At the beginning of the war, the antiwar movement was led primarily by students and developed as an outgrowth of other social movements of the 1960s. The participants in these movements are sometimes referred to as the New Left and the movements themselves as counterculture movements, referring to their opposition to traditional political, economic, and social attitudes. The students who participated in these movements frequently came from middle-class families with educated, liberal parents and often attended top-tier universities such as Berkeley, Michigan, Wisconsin, Harvard, and Columbia.

One of the most influential organizations that emerged from this movement was the Students for a Democratic Society (SDS). Founded in 1960 by students at the University of Michigan, SDS demonstrated in favor of civil rights during the early 1960s, but after President Lyndon B. Johnson initiated Operation Rolling Thunder, the 1965 bombing campaign of North Vietnam, it appeared that he might escalate involvement in Vietnam. In response, on April 17, 1965, SDS sponsored the first antiwar march on Washington, D.C. Although only two thousand marchers were expected, about twenty-five thousand actually protested, making it the largest antiwar protest to be held in Washington, D.C., at that time. As a result of this march, more than three hundred new SDS chapters emerged on campuses across the country, expanding the antiwar movement.

Vietnam Veterans Against the War

In 1967 the scope of those who opposed the war expanded to include Vietnam veterans. Six veterans met at a protest march in New York City and organized the Vietnam Veterans Against the War (VVAW). The VVAW attracted thousands of members over the next four years. One of several protests led by the VVAW was held on January 31, 1971, in a Detroit, Michigan, motel. The VVAW held hearings in what they called the Winter Soldier Investigation. The hearings were held at the same time that Lieutenant William Calley was being court-martialed for atrocities committed by U.S. soldiers under his command at My Lai, a village in southern Vietnam where more than three hundred unarmed civilians, including women and children, were massacred by U.S. troops in March 1968. During the VVAW hearings, more than one hundred witnesses testified that they had committed or witnessed acts of brutality or war crimes in Vietnam. The VVAW condemned U.S. involvement in the war and hoped to demonstrate that the atrocities at My Lai were not an isolated incident.

In April 1971 the VVAW drew national attention with Operation Dewey Canyon III, named after Operation Dewey Canyon II, the February 1971 U.S. invasion of Laos. This protest was held in Washington, D.C., and began on April 19 when veterans and mothers of soldiers killed in Vietnam marched to Arlington National Cemetery. Veteran John Kerry spoke against the war at Senate Foreign Relations Committee hearings, and on the last day, April 23, seven hundred veterans threw their medals and ribbons over the barricade onto the Capitol steps. Although popular support for the war was already waning, protests by veterans further confirmed for many that the government was misrepresenting the events in Vietnam and that U.S. involvement in Vietnam should end. The divide among Americans was widening.

The Whole World Is Watching

Most Vietnam War protests were nonviolent, but when met with force, many turned violent and sometimes deadly. The event that exemplifies the impact of both the media and the antiwar movement on American attitudes toward the Vietnam War occurred in 1968 at the Democratic National Convention in Chicago. The antiwar movement and other organizations of the counterculture movement came head-to-head with the police force of Chicago's Mayor Richard Daley. The year had begun with the Tet Offensive, and for the first time it seemed that the general public was turning away from supporting the war in Vietnam. The campaign year had already been marred by the assassinations of Reverend Martin Luther King Jr. on April 4, and candidate Robert F. Kennedy on June 4, shortly after he won the California Democratic presidential primary. While Democrats gathered at the convention in Chicago, at an August 27 rally with a large media presence, demonstrators chanted, "The whole world's watching." This chant proved to be prophetic and came to symbolize the events of the following day, August 28.

As Hubert Humphrey was being nominated, about three hundred demonstrators prepared to parade to the convention hall. The police asked the demonstrators to disperse, and when they failed to do so, busloads of police reinforcements arrived. While the whole world watched on television, members of the Chicago Police Department waded into the crowd. As demonstrators tried to flee, they were chased and beaten with fists and nightsticks. When the pressure of the fleeing mob forced a ground-floor window of the Chicago Hilton to give way, police followed people who had fallen through the glass into the lounge and beat them.

The police also entered the convention floor, and at least two convention delegates were dragged from the hall by police and beaten. News reporters, photographers, passersby, and members of the clergy were attacked. A grandson of Winston Churchill, there in his capacity as a journalist, was beaten. Anne Kerr, a member of the British Parliament vacationing in Chicago, was maced and taken to jail. Inside the convention center Senator Abraham Ribicoff grabbed the microphone and condemned what he called the "Gestapo tactics" of Mayor Daley and the Chicago Police Department. On the convention floor reporter Dan Rather was shoved around by a group of Mayor Daley's bodyguards, prompting Walter Cronkite to say, on national television, "Dan, it looks like there's a bunch of thugs down there." Before the night was over at least 100 protesters and others had gone to hospital emergency rooms due to injuries sustained at the hands of the police, and 175 were arrested. Because the whole world was in fact watching, the police reaction had the effect of inspiring further support for the antiwar movement.

The Mainstream Protest

In the spring of 1969 the Vietnam Moratorium Committee (VMC) began to arrange a nationwide strike protesting the Vietnam War. The VMC was a moderate organization that appealed to the American mainstream. Supporters included Americans for Democratic Action; the Teamsters; the United Auto Workers; Averell Harriman, President Harry S. Truman's national security adviser during the Korean War; John Kenneth Galbraith, a well-respected economist and political scientist; and twenty-four U.S. senators. On October 15, 1969, millions of people participated in a day of moratorium by not working. The moratorium was the largest nationwide protest in U.S. history.

Despite increasing protest coming from the American mainstream, many in America continued to support U.S. foreign policy in Vietnam. President Nixon and his vice president Spiro T. Agnew made speeches in the 1970s arguing that antiwar protesters were a radical minority and that those who supported his policies in Vietnam were "the great silent majority." Although these speeches did not succeed in swaying public opinion, they did uncover class resentments created by Vietnam. The antiwar movement was led by middle-class Americans and privileged students who were in many cases protected from the draft. The working class served in disproportionate numbers in Vietnam. Many blue-collar Americans grew angry as they watched wealthy college students flouting conventional morality, defying authority, and denouncing the United States. Thus in May 1970 New York construction workers, in what was later learned to be a less-than-spontaneous demonstration of their own, attacked antiwar protesters. Shortly after the demonstration, President Nixon invited the leaders of this group to the White House, where the workers presented Nixon with a hard hat. The "hard hat" worn by construction workers came to symbolize working-class resentment of antiwar protest.

The Tragedy at Kent State

While Nixon may have gained the support of some in the working class, public opinion changed dramatically after the events at Kent State University in Ohio and at Jackson State College in Mississippi. In April 1970 Nixon announced his invasion of Cambodia, and across the nation colleges and universities shut down as a result of student protest. On May 4, 1970, a demonstration was held on the campus of Kent State, and thousands of students gathered to protest. The governor called in the Ohio State National Guard to maintain order. While retreating from a barrage of rocks and bottles thrown by some of the protesters, the Guardsmen stopped and fired into the crowd, killing four students and wounding nine. Two had not even been participants in the demonstration, and none were closer than seventy-five feet from the Guardsmen. Nixon's own Commission on Campus Unrest said of the incident, "The indiscriminate firing of rifles into a crowd of students and the deaths

that followed were unnecessary, unwarranted and inexcusable."
Two weeks after Kent State, another protest took place at Jackson
State College in Mississippi, a predominantly black college. Two
more students were killed, and twelve were wounded. It was discovered later that highway patrolmen and city policemen had fired
nearly four hundred bullets from shotguns, rifles, carbines, and a
submachine gun. The American public was appalled, and the tide
had now turned against U.S. involvement in Vietnam.

Greetings from Your Draft Board

For young American men who turned eighteen during the Vietnam
War, the draft had a tremendous impact. Some have objected to
and resisted the draft in each U.S. war in which it has been instituted, but during the Vietnam War these numbers increased dramatically. In fact, draft resistance became another form of antiwar
protest. Early protesters burned their draft cards, and in response,
on August 31, 1965, President Johnson signed a law criminalizing
draft card burning. Nevertheless, as the war escalated, the public
burning of draft cards continued to grow. By the war's end, three
thousand draft resisters had been imprisoned for burning draft
cards or tampering with draft records.

Before the Tet Offensive, those who hoped to avoid being drafted
took advantage of loopholes in the draft. For example, students enrolled full-time in college were given students deferments, and
members of the National Guard were exempt from the draft, so
many potential draftees enrolled or reenrolled in college or joined
the National Guard. These actions prompted some observers to
argue that only the poor and racial and ethnic minorities were fighting the war. Thus, in January 1966, Johnson abolished automatic
student deferments from the draft.

After the successful North Vietnamese Tet Offensive, the number of those who resisted increased, and the form of draft resistance
changed. Many young men began to either desert or evade the draft
altogether. Although authorities disagree on the exact numbers,
some suggest that about fifty thousand people were actively resist-
ing the war in this way. Others claim that the actual numbers are
probably much higher. Of these, about thirty-two thousand were
military deserters at large in the United States, and twenty-four
thousand had simply refused to report for induction. It is also

believed that 250,000 simply failed to register and were never caught. More than 22,000 Americans were indicted for draft law violations between 1965 and 1975. Of that total, 8,756 were convicted and 4,000 faced imprisonment.

Another way young men resisted the draft was by declaring themselves conscientious objectors. Conscientious objectors are those who on the basis of religious or moral principles refuse to bear arms or participate in military service. Their numbers reached unprecedented proportions in 1972 as mainstream America joined in opposition to the war. Supported by lawyers' organizations and church groups, conscientious objectors fought their cases all the way to the Supreme Court.

Although the older generation, many of whom had served in Korea and World War II, opposed the draft resistance movement, they did agree with young Americans who argued that if young men were old enough to be drafted, they should be able to vote. Nixon signed the Twenty-sixth Amendment in 1971, which reduced the voting age to eighteen years. According to historian Rommel-Ruiz, "Protesters' assertions of being young enough for military service but not old enough to vote had resonated. War demanded public sacrifices; the protesters believed that if they could be drafted to serve the nation, they should be able to influence national politics." The Vietnam War demonstrated the growing political power of young Americans who early in the war dominated the antiwar movement. Having lobbied to reduce the voting age to eighteen, their power and influence would grow.

The Legacy of the Vietnam War

The Vietnam War had a significant impact on those at home, and over the course of the war so changed American attitudes that the American people would look at their government and the nation's role in world affairs in a whole new way. A new term emerged to describe a loss of faith in U.S. leaders. The phrase "credibility gap" expressed the American public's increasing doubts regarding President Johnson's announcements about the Vietnam War and was later expanded to symbolize a general mistrust of the government. "The era of government trust and the rule of experts that signified the 1940s and 1950s was shattered in the late 1960s as the media and antiwar protesters exposed fallacies in national policies," says

Rommel-Ruiz. As a result of this public mistrust, Americans believed less of what politicians said and held them more accountable for what they did.

Another phenomenon emerged as a result of the Vietnam War—what Nixon labeled the "Vietnam Syndrome." After the war Americans were reluctant to support U.S. involvement in foreign wars, especially if the number of U.S. casualties rose above a certain level. The syndrome manifested itself in the public debates over President Ronald Reagan's interventionist policies in Nicaragua and President George H.W. Bush's decision to drive Iraqi forces out of Kuwait. The victory of U.S. forces in the Persian Gulf prompted President Bush to declare in March 1991, "By God, we've kicked the Vietnam syndrome once and for all!" Nevertheless, the fear of intervention appeared again in the debate over President Bill Clinton's commitment of U.S. peacekeeping forces in Somalia and Bosnia. Critics of President George W. Bush's March 2003 decision to invade Iraq often make comparisons to failed strategies employed in Vietnam. Moreover, mistrust of government information led to public debate over the veracity of the intelligence that led to the decision to invade Iraq, particularly intelligence that the regime of Saddam Hussein had developed weapons of mass destruction. Historian Harvard Sitkoff concludes, "A new consensus among foreign policy makers, reflecting the lessons learned from the Vietnam War, became manifest: the United States should use military force only as a last resort; only where the national interest is clearly involved; only when there is strong public support; and only in the likelihood of a relatively quick, inexpensive victory."

For over twenty-five years the Vietnam War has remained in the minds of many Americans. The war had a tremendous impact on the attitudes of the American people and continues to shape the American conscience.

Chapter 1

Taking Steps Toward War

EXAMINING ISSUES THROUGH POLITICAL CARTOONS

Preface

U.S. involvement in Vietnam began long before President Lyndon B. Johnson sent American troops to the Southeast Asian nation in 1965. The foreign policy that led up to Johnson's decision developed during several presidential administrations. Vietnam—part of Indochina, a peninsula of Southeast Asia that also includes Laos, Cambodia, Thailand, Burma, and Malaysia—had been under French colonial rule since the mid-1800s. Because the United States regarded itself as a freed colony, many Americans before World War II empathized with nations such as Vietnam that were struggling to escape colonial rule. However, after World War II, attitudes toward Vietnam became divided. The regime that sought to replace the French colonial government was Communist, and many Americans feared that communism threatened democracy. Thus, some felt threatened by the Communist influence of those who fought for Vietnam's independence, while others believed that as a great democracy, the United States should support Vietnamese self-determination. Among U.S. foreign policy makers, however, the predominant attitude was to oppose independence movements led by Communists.

Harry S. Truman, who succeeded Franklin D. Roosevelt after his death in 1945, shortly before the end of World War II, opposed the Vietnamese independence movement. The League for Vietnamese Independence, also known as the Vietminh, spearheaded that effort, which was led by Communist Ho Chi Minh. After studying and working for Vietnamese independence abroad, Ho Chi Minh had returned to fight the Japanese occupation of Vietnam during World War II. His Vietminh forces fought alongside American soldiers against the Japanese in Southeast Asia. After

World War II ended, Ho Chi Minh, believing the United States would support nations who fought for colonial independence, wrote letters to Truman asking that he support Vietminh efforts to fight French colonial rule. However, Truman's fears about the spread of communism outweighed his interest in supporting these movements.

Global political tensions after World War II added to Truman's fears. World leaders had divided the globe into opposing camps. Joseph Stalin, leader of the Soviet Union, and Mao Zedong, leader of Communist China, envisioned themselves as crusaders for the working class and the peasants, saving the world from oppression by wealthy capitalists. Truman also spoke of two diametrically opposed systems: one free and the other bent on subjugating struggling nations. Western nations envisioned themselves as the champions of freedom and justice, saving the world for democracy. The resulting rivalry came to be known as the Cold War. Responding to these fears, in March 1947 Truman established his policy to contain the spread of communism, known as the Truman Doctrine. Thus, he rejected Ho Chi Minh's request for support and instead authorized $15 million in military aid to the French in 1950, which effectively began U.S. involvement in Vietnam. Over the next four years, the Truman administration would contribute $3 billion and 80 percent of French war supplies. Since Truman failed to support Vietnamese independence, Ho Chi Minh successfully appealed to Communist China for economic and military support. With China's backing, the Vietminh military was transformed into an effective modern army that, under the guidance of General Vo Nguyen Giap, eventually defeated the French in a decisive battle at Dien Bien Phu on May 7, 1954.

Truman's successor, President Dwight D. Eisenhower, also feared the spread of communism and applied the "domino theory" to foreign relations, which in turn influenced his administration's foreign policy toward Vietnam. According to Eisenhower, the fall of one country to communism made it all the easier for the next country to fall to communism. He likened this spread of communism to a row of toppling dominoes. Based on this theory, the United States refused to sign the Geneva Accords, which concluded peace negotiations between France and Vietnam in 1954. The accords stipulated that French colonists would leave Vietnam, that the nation would be divided at the seventeenth parallel, and that free elections would determine the leadership of a unified Vietnam. The United States believed that Ho Chi Minh would win these elections, and now having ties to Communist China, would bring Vietnam under Communist control. Therefore, instead of endorsing the treaty the United States encouraged South Vietnamese president Ngo Dinh Diem, a strong opponent of communism, to hold his own elections. Diem won these elections, then declared South Vietnam independent of North Vietnam, renaming it the Republic of Vietnam. To support South Vietnam, Eisenhower sent financial aid, engineers to reconstruct the nation's infrastructure, and military advisers to train the Army of the Republic of Vietnam.

After coming to office in 1961 President John F. Kennedy continued to send financial aid and advisers to Vietnam. However, internal divisions within Vietnam during his administration complicated efforts to gain American support for aid to Vietnam. Diem was a wealthy Catholic, while most of his people were poor Buddhists. During Diem's attempts to resist the influence of the Communist Vietminh, his secret police tortured and killed thousands of Vietnamese, including Buddhist monks. This strategy backfired as the South Vietnamese people began to turn to the Vietminh for help. The influence of the Vietcong—a group of South Vietnamese rebels that had formed during Eisenhower's administration—grew during Kennedy's administration when these guerrilla warriors sought and received support from the Vietminh. Fearing that Diem was losing control and that South Vietnam might fall to communism, the Kennedy administration implicitly supported a military coup on November 2, 1963, in which Diem was assassinated. To quell dissent and the influence of the Vietcong, Kennedy increased the number of U.S. military advisers in Vietnam to more than sixteen thousand before his assassination on November 22, 1963. Despite the fall of Diem's regime, subsequent regimes failed to stabilize South Vietnam, and the influence of the Vietcong grew.

During the administration of three postwar U.S. presidents—Truman, Eisenhower, and Kennedy—U.S. foreign policy toward Vietnam centered on preventing the spread of communism through economic aid and military advice. In the following chapter the cartoonists consider the effectiveness of America's early steps toward war in Vietnam.

Examining Cartoon 1:
"How Would Another Mistake Help?"

About the Cartoon

After World War II, Communist leaders backed by Communist China began to oppose French colonial rule in Indochina—a peninsula of Southeast Asia comprised of Vietnam, Laos, Cambodia, Thailand, Burma, and Malaysia. The Vietminh, Communists who had opposed the Japanese occupation of Vietnam during World War II, declared Vietnam an independent nation and set up a nationalist government in Hanoi under the leadership of Ho Chi Minh. With financial support from the United States, the French evicted the Vietminh from Hanoi, but the Vietminh fought back fiercely, using guerrilla tactics. The U.S. Congress refused to provide additional military support to the French, and on May 7, 1954, the Vietminh defeated the French at Dien Bien Phu. Over four hundred thousand soldiers and civilians from both sides perished during the struggle.

Published shortly after French defeat, this Pulitzer Prize–winning cartoon by cartoonist Daniel R. Fitzpatrick portrays Uncle Sam, a symbol often used to represent the United States, armed and wading alone into a dark, foreboding swamp labeled "French Mistakes in Indochina." Fitzpatrick suggests that by becoming involved in Vietnam, the United States will repeat the errors made by France. Critics argued that France had gotten bogged down in a costly war that it could not win because it had underestimated the enemy, particularly its use of guerrilla tactics under the direction of General Vo Nguyen Giap. This cartoon suggests that the United States is headed down the same road.

About the Cartoonist

Daniel R. Fitzpatrick was the editorial cartoonist for the *St. Louis Post-Dispatch* for forty-five years, during which time he drew fourteen thousand cartoons. His work, noted for its dark and somber style, won many awards, including the Pulitzer Prize in both 1926 and 1955. He died on May 18, 1969.

Examining Cartoon 2:
"Just Leaned on It a Little . . ."

About the Cartoon

In the cartoon Karl Hubenthal comments on the fall of the Diem regime in South Vietnam. In 1955 Ngo Dinh Diem declared himself president of South Vietnam, which he called the Republic of Vietnam. Corruption within his regime and opposition from South Vietnamese citizens made U.S. support for Diem a controversial policy during the early 1960s. On May 8, 1963, Army of the Republic of Vietnam (ARVN) troops killed nine people when they fired into a crowd of demonstrators protesting the Diem government's discriminatory policies toward Buddhists (Diem was Catholic). In June a Buddhist monk set himself on fire in Saigon in protest. Outraged by the Diem regime's repressive policies and claims that Diem was not vigorously pursuing the war against the Communists, the Kennedy administration indicated to South Vietnamese military leaders that the United States would support a new military government. Diem was assassinated on November 2, 1963, in a military coup backed by the Central Intelligence Agency. Hubenthal uses a shattered Vietnamese artifact to represent the fallen Diem regime. He portrays former president John F. Kennedy like a guilty child caught in the act with lifted shoulders and opened palms, saying "Just Leaned on It a Little," thereby downplaying his role in the coup. Although Diem's regime was weak from internal corruption and thus easily toppled, Kennedy personally approved Diem's ouster.

About the Cartoonist

Karl Hubenthal was hired as a sports cartoonist for the *Los Angeles Herald Examiner* in 1949 and became its chief editorial cartoonist in 1955. Critics claim his political cartoons are more illustrative than "commentative," but Hubenthal took strong, conservative stands on issues such as draft dodgers, anti-Americanism, and military spending during the Vietnam War. Hubenthal won many awards for his cartoons, including seven from the National Cartoonists Society. He died in 1998.

Chapter 2

Going to War:
The Johnson
Years

EXAMINING ISSUES THROUGH
POLITICAL CARTOONS

Preface

A lthough Lyndon B. Johnson demonstrated great leadership in passing civil rights legislation and fighting to end poverty, he is one of the least admired U.S. presidents. Many remember Johnson as the president who escalated the Vietnam War by misleading the American people, creating a new term for a lack of trust in the government—the "credibility gap."

Johnson became president after John F. Kennedy's assassination on November 22, 1963. Johnson's primary goal was to make headway with his Great Society program, which he hoped would end poverty and racial injustice. Johnson did in fact achieve many of his objectives. He pushed through Congress the Civil Rights Act of 1964, which barred discrimination on the basis of race in public accommodations in the United States, authorized the Justice Department to bring suit against states that discriminated against women and minorities, and guaranteed equal opportunities in the workplace. He also oversaw passage of the Voting Rights Act of 1965, which eliminated various barriers to voter registration that white southerners used to restrict African Americans from voting. In addition, under Johnson Congress passed legislation to improve the lives of impoverished Americans, including the Economic Opportunity Act of 1964 and Medicare/Medicaid in 1965. According to African American novelist Ralph Ellison, Johnson was "the greatest American president ever for the poor and the Negroes." These domestic accomplishments were overshadowed, however, by Johnson's actions in Vietnam.

The Gulf of Tonkin incident is an oft-cited example of the way in which Johnson misled the American people to gain support for his foreign policy in Vietnam. On August 4, 1964, two U.S. destroyers reported that they were under attack off the North Vietnamese coast in the Gulf of Tonkin. In response, Johnson ordered retaliatory air strikes against North Vietnamese torpedo boats and oil storage depots. He also asked Congress for a resolution that granted him broad authority to repel armed attacks and to prevent further aggression. The Gulf of Tonkin Resolution won nearly unanimous congressional approval and stood as a symbol of national support for Johnson's foreign policy in Vietnam. The resolution made it possible for Johnson to send U.S. troops to defend South Vietnam. He began sending troops in 1965.

Americans began to question U.S. involvement in Vietnam when they later learned that U.S. naval commanders had reported to Secretary of Defense Robert McNamara that they had difficulty confirming the Gulf of Tonkin attack on U.S. ships. Reports also revealed that Johnson had said to Undersecretary of State George Ball, "Those sailors out there may have been shooting at flying fish." Moreover, the U.S. ships that had purportedly been attacked were conducting electronic espionage. Once these facts were revealed, Johnson's credibility began to wane.

Some scholars claim that if Johnson had encouraged public debate in early 1965 or 1966, a vast majority of Americans would have supported his war efforts. People were frustrated by the seemingly endless and bloody war in Vietnam, however, and the failure to conduct public debate led many to believe that the president had something to hide concerning America's involvement. The credibility gap deepened as Johnson escalated the war, sending increasing numbers of troops. To justify this escalation, Johnson and his advisers provided only part of the truth when discussing U.S. strategy and tactics in Vietnam with the public. Questions went unanswered, and information about the course of the war was minimal.

One strategy used to explain the progress of the war was the body count. Vietnam had become a war of attrition, in which the strategy was to kill more North Vietnamese Army and Vietcong (NVA/VC) soldiers in South Vietnam than the NVA/VC could easily replace. Thus body counts, strategists believed, helped determine whether the United States was winning the war. However, body counts were highly inaccurate; some officers inflated their body counts to advance their careers, while others simply guessed because guerrilla warfare in the jungles of Vietnam made counting bodies difficult. Nevertheless, the Johnson administration reported high NVA/VC body counts as evidence that the United States was winning the war. In 1967, however, members of the media began questioning the accuracy of the high NVA/VC body counts. The NVA/VC continued to withstand U.S. military efforts as Johnson sent more troops to Vietnam. If the NVA/VC were able to match these efforts, the media reasoned, then the NVA/VC body counts must be much lower than the Johnson administration was reporting. Thus, some suspected that Johnson was misleading the public and that the United States was not winning the war in Vietnam.

To counteract the growing credibility gap, which was partly the result of questionable body counts, in November 1967 Johnson was advised to emphasize military progress rather than battles and losses when discussing the war with the media. Johnson declared that the United States could see "light at the end of the tunnel," which became the signature quote of the Vietnam War during his administration. The strategy was initially effective, and approval of Johnson's Vietnam policy rose. The credibility gap turned into a chasm, however, on January 31, 1968. The NVA/VC launched the Tet (New Year) Offensive, attacking over one hundred South Vietnamese cities. American combat deaths skyrocketed and reached a peak of twelve hundred per month, and the phrase "light at the end of the tunnel" became a bitter joke. Dissent in the United States grew, and Johnson decided not to run for reelection in 1968.

According to historian Robert Dallek, "Lyndon Johnson's escalation of the war in Vietnam divided Americans into warring camps, had cost 30,000 American lives by the time he left office, destroyed Johnson's presidency, and blocked further domestic reform, Johnson's principal goal."

Although in time Johnson's accomplishments received recognition, he is primarily remembered for his foreign policy decisions in Vietnam. In the following chapter the cartoonists examine the nature and scope of Johnson's policies in Vietnam as well as the public's reaction.

Examining Cartoon 1:
"We've Got to Operate, and Fast!"

"We've got to operate, and fast!"

About the Cartoon

President Lyndon B. Johnson, Secretary of Defense Robert Mc-Namara, and Secretary of State Dean Rusk were the chief architects of the Vietnam War during Johnson's administration (1963–1969). Johnson, McNamara, and Rusk viewed communism as a threat to democracy and feared that if the United States did not protect South Vietnam from takeover by Communist North Vietnam, communism would spread throughout Southeast Asia and beyond. Thus, in 1965 Johnson sent troops to defend South Vietnam. Pierre Bellocq captures the Johnson administration's desire to protect Vietnam in this cartoon. Johnson, McNamara, and Rusk are portrayed as emergency-room doctors trying to save the patient —Vietnam. The X-ray of Vietnam appears to be ravaged by dark tumors, presumably representing communism. Johnson articulates the urgency of the situation, saying, "We've got to operate, and fast!" Bellocq implies that the need to save Vietnam is more urgent than the need to save the Dominican Republic, whose dark spots are much smaller. Johnson had already sent U.S. military forces to the Dominican Republic under the pretense of "protecting American lives," although it was later discovered that the real fear was of a Communist takeover. This deceit created a rift between the administration, the American media, and the American people that was to deepen as the Vietnam War escalated.

About the Cartoonist

French-born Pierre Bellocq is an illustrator and an editorial cartoonist. Bellocq, formerly an amateur horse racer, is currently the cartoonist for the *Daily Racing Form* under the pseudonym PEB. In 1999 Bellocq won a National Cartoonists Society award for newspaper illustration.

Examining Cartoon 2:
"The Strategists"

About the Cartoon

Some analysts claim that President Lyndon B. Johnson had great skill in crafting decisions that offered up something for everyone. His Vietnam strategies included increased bombing raids to appease the "hawks," those that prefer aggressive military strategies, while intermittent efforts at negotiation were designed to please the "doves," those who prefer nonmilitary strategies. Others claim, however, that Johnson's efforts to build a consensus and appease everyone often meant that he avoided making difficult, but more effective decisions about American involvement in Vietnam. Cartoonist Bill Mauldin illustrates the flaws in the two primary strategies that Johnson was being asked to take in Vietnam. The military position, portrayed by a soldier, was to escalate the war and go for victory. The cartoon indicates, however, that this strategy is based on "rickety" ideas, as seen in the poorly constructed stairs he is ascending. Moreover, the stairs—hence the strategy—appear to be going nowhere. The robed man in sandals represents the strategy of antiwar activists. This figure recommends that the United States get out of Vietnam. Antiwar activists claimed that Vietnam was involved in a civil war that was not the concern of the United States. Because his head is buried in the sand, the cartoon suggests that this strategy ignores the reality of Communist expansion. Because neither character can see, Mauldin implies that neither side really knows the outcome of its own strategy.

About the Cartoonist

Bill Mauldin was an editorial cartoonist for the *St. Louis Post-Dispatch* and later the *Chicago Sun-Times*. Mauldin won a Pulitzer Prize in 1945 for a book of "Willie and Joe" cartoons and again in 1959.

Examining Cartoon 3:

"...But You Should Have Seen Rodney Biting the Cop..."

"...BUT YOU SHOULD HAVE SEEN RODNEY BITING THE COP IN THE CALF...AND HE NEVER LET GO!"

About the Cartoon

Students began to protest at American universities nationwide shortly after President Lyndon B. Johnson sent troops to Vietnam. Mobilization committees, named for their efforts to mobilize people to demonstrate, often organized these protests. Edmund S. Valtman illustrates his disapproval of student antiwar protesters in this cartoon, which portrays a mobilization committee office after a demonstration. Valtman's representation of these students is not flattering. The students are slovenly and ill kempt, wearing attire that at the time was considered unconventional. For example, long hair on men represented resistance to authority, and short skirts on women implied loose morality. One buxom woman is even buck-toothed, indicating she lacks intelligence. Valtman also hints that the students may themselves have Communist ideals because they appear to have read Karl Marx's treatise on the evils of capitalism, *Das Kapital*, which is lying on the desk. Valtman's most direct criticism targets what he believes to be the hypocrisy of antiwar protesters, who behave violently while at the same time claiming to want peace. Although the bandaged figure, Rodney, appears to have been beaten during a recent demonstration, he grins as the young woman at his side says, "But you should have seen Rodney biting the cop in the calf . . . and he never let go!"

About the Cartoonist

Edmund S. Valtman, a native of Estonia, came to the United States when the Soviets reoccupied the nation after World War II. His experience with Soviet communism shaped the anti-Communist stance in his cartoons. He joined the *Hartford Times* as editorial cartoonist in 1951. He received the National Safety Council award in 1958 and a Pulitzer Prize for cartooning in 1962. Valtman became a U.S. citizen in 1959.

Examining Cartoon 4:

"You'll Have to Economize by Doing Some Pruning!"

About the Cartoon

Richard Yardley questions President Lyndon B. Johnson's judgment on government spending on domestic and foreign affairs in the cartoon. Johnson, who often appeared in a cowboy hat, was from Texas. Thus Yardley uses a colossal cactus to portray government spending. One enormous branch represents the costs of Johnson's "Great Society," a program Johnson hoped would end poverty, promote equality, improve education, rejuvenate cities, and protect the environment. The other massive branch signifies the costs of escalating the Vietnam War. According to Yardley, asking federal agency heads to trim their small budgets—dwarfed by the costs of Johnson's budget needs—will do little to reduce the overall budget. While Johnson and the agency heads are focusing on the small branches at the bottom of the cactus, all the other characters—including a child and several animals—are looking up and can clearly see the folly of Johnson's request. Before Johnson left office, even his plans for a "Great Society" were dwarfed by Vietnam War spending.

About the Cartoonist

Richard Yardley was the editorial cartoonist for the *Baltimore Sun*. According to one commentator, Yardley mocked sin but never condemned the sinners and often saw events in a more fantastic sense, having more in common with the children's book illustrator Dr. Seuss than the dark, philosophical editorial cartoonists of his day. He died in 1979.

Chapter 3

The Long Road to Peace: The Nixon Years

Preface

During the presidential campaign of 1968 Richard Nixon focused on restoring "law and order" to a nation that appeared to be coming unraveled. America was seriously divided on the Vietnam War, and antiwar protesters and hecklers dogged the presidential candidates. Nixon remained relatively silent on the issue, saying that he wanted the peace talks being negotiated at the time to succeed. He added only that he had a secret plan to achieve an honorable peace in Southeast Asia and withdraw American troops from Vietnam. After being elected president, Nixon revealed his "Vietnamization" plan on June 8, 1969. Vietnamization was the label Nixon gave to his process of phasing out U.S. forces and turning the responsibility for the war over to the South Vietnamese. To achieve this goal, the United States would provide military equipment and training to improve the effectiveness of the South Vietnamese army, the Army of the Republic of Vietnam (ARVN). Although Nixon's peace plan was achieved during his second term, it was a long, controversial process. The North Vietnamese were not the only obstacle to peace. Nixon also had to overcome antiwar activists and the fears of the president of South Vietnam, Nguyen Van Thieu.

The antiwar movement proved to be a significant obstacle on Nixon's road to peace. Because the antiwar movement in America had become so strong, the North Vietnamese concluded that internal pressure would force the United States to withdraw, even if North Vietnam refused to negotiate a peace with South Vietnam. Nixon responded to North Vietnam's failure to negotiate by extensive bombing of North Vietnamese Army (NVA) strongholds in Cambodia in February and March 1969. The bombing was done secretly, however, because Cambodia was considered a neutral country.

The strategy backfired in America. Although Nixon had withdrawn twenty-five thousand U.S. troops by the time the secret bombing was revealed, antiwar activists became further aggravated.

Frustrated by the antiwar movement's objection to his plan, Nixon appealed to what he called "the silent majority." Antiwar activists were the minority, he claimed. The majority of Americans, Nixon believed, supported his policies. Thus when critics opposed the bombing of Cambodia, Nixon appealed to the American people in a controversial speech delivered on November 3, 1969. In this speech Nixon explained his plans for "peace with honor," which meant that both the United States and North Vietnam would withdraw from South Vietnam. If the United States withdrew unilaterally, he warned, the world would believe that America could not defend its allies, and violence would break out worldwide.

This speech only temporarily derailed the antiwar movement, which again gained ground in the spring of 1970. Nixon responded by withdrawing 150,000 U.S. troops. However, fearing a massive NVA assault in response to these troop withdrawals, Nixon authorized the invasion of Cambodia by U.S. and ARVN forces. In response, protests erupted on campuses nationwide, culminating in the tragic death of four students on the Kent State University campus in Ohio after National Guardsmen opened fire on a crowd of protesters. As a result the antiwar movement gained even further ground. These deaths created another firestorm of protest, and riots erupted across the nation. Despite antiwar sentiment, military authorities claimed that the invasion of Cambodia was in fact a military success. U.S. and ARVN forces captured tons of military equipment and stalled Soviet and Chinese efforts to send more equipment. Moreover, the ARVN had fought well, an encouraging sign that Vietnamization might work.

During the summer of 1972, Henry Kissinger, Nixon's national security adviser and representative in the peace talks, advised Nixon that the North Vietnamese showed signs that they might be willing to negotiate. The Soviets and the Chinese were providing less aid to North Vietnam, and the ARVN was fighting well. In October the North Vietnamese offered reasonable terms, and a tentative cease-fire agreement was reached. The agreement stipulated that the United States withdraw its troops, that both sides exchange prisoners of war, and that the North Vietnamese send no further troops into the South. When Kissinger visited Thieu to discuss the peace proposal, Thieu adamantly opposed allowing North Vietnamese troops to remain indefinitely in South Vietnam and publicly denounced the peace proposal. Thus Thieu proved to be one of Nixon's last obstacles to peace. Nixon explained to Thieu that to remove all NVA troops was impractical. To appease Thieu, Nixon promised that the United States would not permit a Communist takeover.

In October 1972, peace appeared to be at hand, but Nixon faced one more obstacle. The North Vietnamese decided to stall on their own cease-fire terms. Both Nixon and Kissinger were furious. Nixon retaliated with another intense bombing campaign during the Christmas holiday in 1972. Although controversial, this strategy worked, and in January 1973 the North Vietnamese decided to negotiate. A cease-fire was officially declared on January 27, 1973. The United States would not be able to keep its promise to prevent a Communist takeover, however. The South Vietnamese government surrendered to the Communist North in April 1975.

Scholars continue to debate the effectiveness of Nixon's Vietnamization plan. In the following chapter cartoonists examine this and other policies implemented by the Nixon administration along the long road to peace.

Examining Cartoon 1:
"I Told You I'd Get You Out of Vietnam"

"I never did say how, but I told you I'd get you out of Vietnam."

About the Cartoon

One of Richard Nixon's 1968 campaign promises was that he had a secret plan to achieve an honorable peace in Southeast Asia and withdraw American troops from Vietnam. Once elected, he revealed his secret plan, which he called Vietnamization. While he withdrew U.S. troops, Nixon planned to shift responsibility for the war to the South Vietnamese army. Nixon did begin to withdraw troops. Some of his "peace" policies, however, actually escalated the war. In March 1969, shortly after his inauguration, Nixon launched Operation Menu, a series of secret air strikes against Vietminh and Vietcong targets in Cambodia, a nation bordering Vietnam, and on April 29, 1970, American troops invaded Cambodia.

In this cartoon John Fischetti objects to the insincerity of Nixon's campaign promise and the dishonesty of his Vietnamization plan. Fischetti mocks Nixon's campaign promise by having Nixon justify his actions, saying, "I never did say how, but I told you I'd get you out of Vietnam" as he and a weary U.S. soldier wade through the swamps from Vietnam to Cambodia. Fischetti also criticizes Nixon's Vietnamization plan by showing Nixon "holding up" the head of a South Vietnamese soldier. This suggests that even Nixon knows that the South Vietnamese are incapable of defending themselves on their own. The cartoonist insinuates that Nixon's plans are misleading and that he should not be trusted.

About the Cartoonist

John Fischetti, who died in 1980, was a Pulitzer Prize–winning editorial cartoonist whose work appeared in the *New York Herald*, the *Chicago Daily News*, and the *Chicago Sun-Times*.

Examining Cartoon 2:

"You Won a Lottery—What's the Prize?"

"YOU WON A LOTTERY—WHAT'S THE PRIZE?"

About the Cartoon

On December 1, 1969, the nation held the first draft lottery since 1942. A large glass container held 366 blue plastic capsules containing every possible birth date. People nationwide listened on the radio and watched on television as each capsule was drawn. The date within the first capsule drawn was September 14, so all men born on September 14 in any year between 1944 and 1950 were assigned lottery number one. The drawing continued until all days of the year had been assigned. After the lottery, draftees were called for duty in order of their draft number, beginning with number one and continuing until the military's manpower needs were met. Thus, if a young man were born on a date assigned a low number in the lottery, he would likely be drafted; if he drew a high number, he would not.

Appearing the day after the lottery, the cartoon by Don Wright points out the irony of calling the selection of military draftees a lottery, particularly during the Vietnam War, when young soldiers were dying. The stunned young man in the cartoon holds a letter from his local draft board that orders him into service, identifiable by the infamous salutation "Greetings." The boy's mother, unaware of the meaning of this particular "lottery," clasps her hands in joy at the prospect that her son had won, and asks, "What's the prize?" President Richard Nixon, who had instituted the lottery, ended the draft in July 1973.

About the Cartoonist

Pulitzer Prize–winning cartoonist Don Wright began his career as an editorial cartoonist in 1963. He currently works for the *Palm Beach Post*.

Examining Cartoon 3:
"Pornography"

About the Cartoon

During the 1968 presidential campaign, Richard Nixon promised to achieve an honorable peace in Vietnam. Once elected, Nixon began peace talks with North Vietnam. However, whenever peace talks failed, the United States escalated the bombing of North Vietnam, actions that drew harsh criticism. Nixon made a televised address to defend his strategy, asking America to unite in seeking "not the peace of surrender, but peace with honor."

Scott Long parodies Nixon's strategy by portraying the massive bombing of North Vietnam as a long-running pornographic movie titled *Peace with Honor*. Long portrays the strategy as lurid and sensational with plenty of dope, blood, and "stuff" to please those who enjoy such fare, presumably the nation's "hawks." The movie has received reviews by major newspapers that call it "Incredible!" and "Shocking!" The movie's stars include General Nguyen Van Thieu, president of South Vietnam; General Nguyen Cao Ky, vice president of South Vietnam; Ellsworth Bunker, U.S. ambassador to South Vietnam; U.S. secretary of defense Mel Laird; National Security Adviser Henry Kissinger; the Joint Chiefs of Staff of the U.S. military; and the nameless South Vietnamese guerrilla rebels, the Vietcong, also known as V.C. To illustrate his point that this bombing strategy is nothing new, Long's movie poster indicates that the movie has been running continuously since 1965. Although the movie is rated "X," Long suggests that everyone—adults and children—can see it because although the movie is pornographic, the war in Vietnam is, of course, quite real.

About the Cartoonist

Scott Long was editorial cartoonist for the *Minneapolis Tribune*.

Examining Cartoon 4:
"Last Rites"

LAST RITES

About the Cartoon

When Americans learned that U.S. troops had invaded Cambodia, antiwar protesters organized demonstrations at campuses nation-wide. On May 4, 1970, a demonstration was held on the campus of Kent State University in Ohio. Thousands of students gathered to protest, and some threw rocks and bottles at Ohio State National Guardsmen that the governor had called to maintain order. For reasons that remain unclear, while retreating the barrage, guardsmen stopped and fired into the crowd for thirteen seconds, killing four students and wounding nine. A July 1970 FBI investigation recommended that six guardsmen be prosecuted. Nevertheless, an Ohio state grand jury concluded in August 1970 that the guardsmen's actions were justified. President Nixon appointed a commission, led by former governor of Pennsylvania William Scranton, to look into the events at Kent State. The Scranton commission issued a report in September 1970 that concluded the deaths were "unnecessary, unwarranted and inexcusable." In October 1970, demands for a federal grand jury mounted. On August 13, 1971, however, Attorney General John Mitchell closed the case, dismissing allegations against the guardsmen as not credible, claiming "there is no likelihood of successful prosecutions of individual Guardsmen."

In this cartoon Herblock concludes that by closing the case, Mitchell has performed "Last Rites" on the investigation, thus burying any hope of learning the truth about what really happened and achieving justice for the victims. Mitchell casually discards gloves he wore to bury the matter so that he would not get his hands dirty, suggesting that he did not want the administration to be sullied by the truth. For many analysts, the killings at Kent State represent a major turning point in American attitudes toward the Vietnam War and the judgment of the nation's president, Richard Nixon.

About the Cartoonist

Herbert Block, better known by his pseudonym "Herblock," was a multi–award winning editorial cartoonist who worked for the *Washington Post* from 1945 until his death in 2001. His collections include *Herblock on All Fronts* and *Herblock's State of the Union*.

Examining Cartoon 5:
"A Muted Peace Concerto"

About the Cartoon

Nixon's attempt to achieve peace in Vietnam began in February 1970 when his national security adviser, Henry Kissinger, began secret meetings with North Vietnamese negotiator Le Duc Tho. Little progress was made until the summer of 1972. To promote an agreement, Kissinger assured North Vietnam that its troops could remain in South Vietnam after the cease-fire. In return, North Vietnam withdrew its condition that South Vietnamese president Nguyen Van Thieu be removed and agreed to stop sending troops to South Vietnam. By October 1972 a tentative cease-fire agreement was reached. Nixon proudly announced the withdrawal of U.S. troops, freedom for American POWs, and settlement of South Vietnam's future. However, when Kissinger visited Thieu to discuss the peace proposal, Thieu adamantly opposed allowing North Vietnamese troops to remain indefinitely in South Vietnam and publicly denounced the peace proposal.

In the cartoon Ranan Lurie satirizes Nixon's efforts to achieve peace in Vietnam. Lurie depicts Nixon as a soloist performing a concerto, a musical composition written for a solo instrument that is to be performed with an orchestra. Nixon wears the striped pants and vest of Uncle Sam, often used to represent the United States. However, Nixon needed an orchestra of others to cooperate if he was to successfully achieve peace. In October 1972, as the peace concerto neared its conclusion, South Vietnam's President Nguyen Van Thieu, whom Lurie portrays as a cork in Nixon's instrument, blocked Nixon's peace efforts.

About the Cartoonist

Ranan Lurie came to the United States from his native Israel in 1968. He was *Life* magazine's first and only political cartoonist. Lurie served for three years as political cartoonist and contributing editor for *Newsweek* and senior analyst and political cartoonist for *U.S. News & World Report*. In September 2000 he joined *Foreign Affairs*. He has published ten books of his cartoons and has won numerous awards.

Chapter 4

The Legacy of
the Vietnam War

EXAMINING ISSUES THROUGH
POLITICAL CARTOONS

Preface

American involvement in Vietnam stimulates emotionally charged debate. While most agree that U.S. intervention in Vietnam was a tragic failure, scholars continue to dispute whether the intervention was justified. Some argue that American leaders sincerely believed communism was a worldwide threat and that protecting nations such as South Vietnam from Communist takeover was the prevailing U.S. foreign policy at the time. Others claim that the theories used to justify U.S. intervention in Vietnam were flawed and that American involvement was immoral.

The decision to defend South Vietnam from attack by the Communist North was in harmony with previous U.S. foreign policy decisions. Protecting pro-Western nations was a U.S. foreign policy pattern. The United States had protected West Berlin and South Korea when they were threatened with Communist takeover. Thus protecting South Vietnam was consistent with U.S. foreign policy.

Several factors contributed to the decision to intervene in Vietnam. Although some of these reasons are not as compelling in light of the information available today, at the time leaders believed they were reasonable assumptions. The primary reason for U.S. intervention was the belief in a monolithic Communist threat. U.S. policy makers believed that the Soviet Union and Communist China were working together to spread communism worldwide. Later it was revealed that Sino-Soviet relations were often in conflict. The Chinese believed that Communist nations should take a strong stand against "imperialist" nations such as the United States. The Soviets, on the other hand, realized that capitalism was not going to crumble as quickly as they had originally expected. In fact, the United States was getting stronger both economically and militarily.

This realization, as well as the threat of nuclear war, prompted the Soviets to take a less aggressive approach. Unaware of the animosity between Communist China and the Soviet Union, U.S. leaders believed that China, with the help of the Soviets, was encouraging and assisting North Vietnam to attack the South as part of a master plan to take over Asia. The Soviet Union, analysts later learned, supported North Vietnam primarily to protect its interests against the Communist Chinese, not in a unified front against the United States.

The United States also believed Soviet premier Nikita Khrushchev when he said the Soviet Union would support "wars of national liberation." Since supporting Communist revolutions in industrial societies was too costly, the Soviet Union thought it would be easier to do so in developing nations. John F. Kennedy's administration believed that Vietnam was a test case and thus hoped to thwart Communist influence. For this reason it was also important to prove the success of Western economic and social development in Vietnam. Thus early intervention in Vietnam involved social and economic development strategies in addition to military support.

Another reason given for American involvement in Vietnam was that U.S. leaders did not want to repeat what was referred to as Harry S. Truman's mistake in China. The United States had failed to intervene to prevent the Communists from coming to power in China in 1949. Although Secretary of State Dean Acheson had claimed that the civil war in China was beyond the control of the U.S. government, Truman was blamed for losing China to communism. Thus, Democrats such as John F. Kennedy and Lyndon B. Johnson were reluctant to lose another Asian country to communism because of American inaction. Security analyst Benjamin Frankel concludes:

What we now know about the brittleness of the international communist movement and its internal divisions . . . makes it hard to see the events in Southeast Asia through the eyes of decisionmakers at the time. Yet, to make sense of the U.S. decisions regarding the war, one must take their point of view. Their thinking was not unreasonable for the time and was consistent with the assumptions sustaining U.S. foreign policy as a whole.

Other analysts disagree with these conclusions. They claim that U.S. intervention, not Communist aggression by North Vietnam, divided the nation; thus U.S. involvement created the conflict in Vietnam. Ho Chi Minh, the leader of the Vietminh, fought for the independence of the entire nation of Vietnam, not North Vietnam alone. After the Vietminh defeated the French in 1954, the Geneva Accords stipulated nationwide elections to reunify the country. Because the United States knew that Communist Ho Chi Minh would likely win these elections, it refused to agree to the Geneva Accords. Instead, the United States supported an unpopular anti-Communist government in South Vietnam that divided the nation.

Another reason cited to justify American involvement in Vietnam is that the United States was protecting international order and Vietnamese human rights consistent with the "just war" philosophy. Critics of the Vietnam War claim that U.S. behavior in Vietnam proved that these were not the nation's true motives. The United States in fact blocked the democratic process by preventing nationwide elections that would have united Vietnam. The United States was the aggressor because it supported an unpopular regime in the South in an effort to keep Vietnam divided. Moreover, the regimes supported by the United States tortured and killed many South Vietnamese people. According to political scientist Jerome Slater, "Far from serving the purposes of nonaggression, freedom, democracy, or self-determination in Vietnam, the United States made a mockery of these principles. As in so many other places during the cold war, whenever ideological anticommunism clashed with morality, there was no contest."

Another argument against U.S. intervention in Vietnam is the principle of proportionality. This principle holds that the good that comes from war must outweigh the damage of war itself. For some analysts the Vietnam War was a tragic example of the failure of proportionality. Commentators such as Slater suggest that U.S. leaders themselves knew that the harm of war outweighed the good that would result. He questions why the United States did not apply even greater force in Vietnam if leaders believed in the apocalyptic predictions of the domino theory, which predicted that if one nation in Southeast Asia were to fall to communism, other nations would also fall. This unwillingness to escalate the U.S. commitment to the level that might bring victory suggests that American decision makers had doubts. Instead, U.S. intervention in Vietnam needlessly sacrificed the lives of American and Vietnamese soldiers and countless civilians.

Many believe American intervention in Vietnam was a gross, if not criminal, violation of the principle *jus in bello* (justice in war). This principle holds that war must never be made upon innocent civilians. Many critics believe that the violation of this principle was the worst feature of the Vietnam War. The strategy of the war was attrition. General William C. Westmoreland, commander of U.S. forces in Vietnam, said, "We'll just go on bleeding them until Hanoi wakes up to the fact that they have bled their country to the point of national disaster for generations." Because the United States used massive, indiscriminate firepower, and because the enemy blended into the general population, North and South Vietnamese civilians inevitably suffered. In addition, U.S. policy dictated the deliberate destruction of villages and farmland in South Vietnam to deprive Communists of bases from which to conduct war. Thus, says Slater, "Vietnam itself became increasingly unimportant. Rather, it became a battlefield in the global ideological crusade against 'international communism,' a country that—regrettably —had to be destroyed in order to be saved."

Scholars still question U.S. military intervention in Vietnam and the impact the war had on both the Vietnamese and the American people. The cartoons in the following chapter explore the legacy of the Vietnam War.

Examining Cartoon 1:
"Anyone Care to Give Again to Vietnam . . .?"

"Anyone care to give again to Vietnam . . . ?"

About the Cartoon

In this cartoon Pat Oliphant reveals the reaction many Americans had to President Gerald Ford's request that Congress give more economic and military aid to South Vietnam. In order to save face in the eyes of the world and keep former president Richard Nixon's promise to help South Vietnam, conservatives encouraged Ford to request the aid. However, many Americans wanted to wash their hands of Vietnam, believing that the United States had already sacrificed enough. To illustrate this attitude, Oliphant portrays President Ford carrying a donation can, asking, "Anyone care to give again to Vietnam . . .?" The expressions on the faces of the group of angry and disgusted Americans he passes illustrates that most Americans felt they had already paid enough. In the early years of U.S. involvement in Vietnam, the younger generation made up the greatest percentage of those who opposed intervention. As the cartoon shows, by 1975, the old and young were unified in their opposition to U.S. involvement, so much so that the old man threatens to throw a brick at Ford and the child a rock. Oliphant's cartoon also represents the attitude of frustrated Vietnam veterans, who had already made great sacrifices in Vietnam yet received little support on their return. Of the more than 2 million Americans who went to Vietnam, 300,000 were physically wounded and many more bore psychological scars, yet virtually nothing was done to help these veterans adjust. Although most veterans succeeded in making the transition to ordinary civilian life, many did not. More Vietnam veterans committed suicide after the war than had died in it. As many as 750,000 became homeless. Nearly 700,000 draftees had received less than honorable discharges, which prevented their getting education and medical benefits. Many of these veterans were poor, badly educated, and nonwhite, thus they found it difficult to get and keep jobs, to maintain family relationships, and to stay out of jail. Although many believed these dysfunctional veterans needed support and medical attention, the Veterans Administration was reluctant to admit the special difficulties they faced and their need for additional benefits. In the face of this treatment, Oliphant reasons, asking Vietnam veterans to give tax dollars to support South Vietnam is absurd. Congress, in fact, rejected the request.

About the Cartoonist

Pat Oliphant is a native of Australia who moved to the United States in 1964 to become editorial cartoonist for the *Denver Post*. He moved to the *Washington Star* in 1975, then became an independent syndicated cartoonist; his work appears in five hundred newspapers in the United States and other countries. He has won several awards, including a 1967 Pulitzer Prize.

Examining Cartoon 2:

"Images from the Fall of Saigon"

About the Cartoon

G.B. Trudeau reflects the despair felt by many Americans upon learning that South Vietnamese president Duong Van Minh had surrendered the Saigon government and its military forces to the Vietcong on April 30, 1975. Phred, pictured in the first frame, and B.D., pictured in the last frame, are recurring characters in Trudeau's strip *Doonesbury*. Phred is always dressed in the black pajamas worn by Vietcong soldiers, and B.D., who is identified by the football helmet he wears, is a conservative American who served in Vietnam, where he met Phred. Phred's role in the strip is to reveal the folly of U.S. involvement in Vietnam to B.D., who despite Phred's efforts continues to believe U.S. actions in Vietnam are justified. In the strip, Trudeau shows Phred in Saigon penning a letter to his mother, the starred flag of Communist North Vietnam flying overhead. The images in the second and third frame are reproduced from actual photos published in U.S. newspapers at the time. In the second frame, mobs of South Vietnamese attempt to scale the wall of the U.S. embassy in Saigon, hoping to get to the helicopter pickup zone. The third frame shows Americans climbing stairs to a makeshift helipad. The last frame shows that B.D. has in fact seen these images and is devastated. Phred's open-ended question, "I wonder what my former adversary, B.D., must have felt?" and the distressing photos of the last days of Saigon suggest that in Trudeau's opinion, many Americans felt that the fall of Saigon was a great tragedy.

About the Cartoonist

Garry, or G.B., Trudeau began his cartooning career while attending Yale University; his *Doonesbury* comic strip evolved from his *Bull Tales* strip for the student newspaper. *Doonesbury*, nationally syndicated since 1970, appears in hundreds of newspapers. Trudeau has also written and produced plays and television programs. He won the Pulitzer Prize for Editorial Cartooning in 1975.

Examining Cartoon 3:
"Vietnamese, Stay Away from Our Town"

"Some Of Them Must Wish We Had Stayed Away From THEIR Towns"

About the Cartoon

In April 1975, as the city of Saigon in South Vietnam fell to the Communists, some 135,000 Vietnamese refugees fled to America. This first group of refugees was comprised mainly of ex-military and government officials who had worked for the United States during the war and their families. Initially, they came to U.S. military bases in California, Arkansas, Pennsylvania, and Florida, eventually settling elsewhere. Vietnamese refugees were initially not welcomed by many Americans. A poll taken in 1975 showed only 36 percent were in favor of Vietnamese immigration. President Gerald Ford and other officials, however, strongly supported the refugees and passed the Indochina Migration and Refugee Act in 1975, which allowed them to enter the United States under a special status. In order to prevent the refugees from forming ethnic enclaves and to minimize their impact on local communities, they were scattered all over the country. Within a few years, however, most resettled in California and Texas, giving those states the largest Vietnamese American populations.

In this cartoon, Herblock questions the reasoning of those Americans who oppose allowing Vietnamese refugees to settle in their cities and towns. He suggests that opponents ignore or have forgotten the impact U.S. military intervention had on the Vietnamese people. To illustrate, Herblock portrays a man carrying a sign that protests the arrival of Vietnamese refugees, demanding, "VIETNAMESE, STAY AWAY FROM OUR TOWN," as a Vietnamese family living in a refugee camp looks on. Another man attempts to remind the protester of the horrors faced by the Vietnamese as a result of U.S. intervention, saying, "Some Of Them Must Wish We Had Stayed Away From THEIR Towns." He holds a newspaper with a commonly seen image of a terrified, naked Vietnamese child and its mother fleeing a village destroyed by napalm, an incendiary agent that could be dropped from airplanes. It was a practice during the Vietnam War to destroy Vietnamese villages with napalm so that Vietcong guerrillas would have no place to hide. This representation is also reminiscent of Nick Ut's Pulitzer Prize–winning photo of nine-year-old Kim Phuc seen fleeing her Vietnamese village in terror with her arms outstretched, her naked body burned by napalm. Herblock concludes that the Vietnamese suffered more from U.S. involvement in Vietnam than Americans would suffer from Vietnamese immigration to America.

About the Cartoonist

Herbert Block, better known by his pseudonym "Herblock," was a multi–award winning editorial cartoonist who worked for the *Washington Post* from 1945 until his death in 2001. Prior to that he drew cartoons for the *Chicago Daily News* and the Newspaper Enterprise Association (NEA), as well as for the U.S. Army during World War II. His collections include *Herblock on All Fronts* and *Herblock's State of the Union*.

Examining Cartoon 4:
"Old Myths Home"

'Hi, everybody! Look who's here!'

About the Cartoon

In the cartoon Doug Marlette lampoons the arguments that U.S. leaders used to justify America's continued involvement in Vietnam. He portrays these arguments as myths that have gone to an "Old Myths Home" to retire, suggesting that each of them has been proven wrong. Shortly after World War II, Harry S. Truman's administration claimed that the United States needed to protect democratic nations such as South Vietnam from monolithic communism. Marlette presents this myth as a three-headed dragon: The head with a starred cap represents Communist China, the bear head represents the Soviet Union, and the head with the conical rice hat and goatee is Vietnam. The idea of a unified Communist force appeared in NSC-68, a U.S. foreign policy document of 1950, which argued that communism was a monolithic force bent on world domination. It stressed the need to confront Communists anywhere in the world at any cost. Thus it was used to support American involvement in Vietnam. This myth was dispelled, however, when the United States learned that Sino-Soviet relations were in fact uneasy. The Soviet Union and China had different ideas about the purpose of communism and the direction it should take. China even accused the Soviet Union of going soft on capitalism. Moreover, Ho Chi Minh, the leader of the Communist Vietminh, only sought help from China because the United States refused to help fight French colonial rule.

Another retired myth is the Domino Theory. To justify his support for South Vietnam, President Dwight Eisenhower put forward this theory. He argued that if Communists took South Vietnam, then the other countries in the region such as Laos, Cambodia, Thailand, Burma, Malaysia, and Indonesia, would follow like dominoes arranged in a row. South Vietnam eventually did fall in 1975 but with few of the consequences predicted by the domino theory. Southeast Asia, like other regions in the world, is composed of both Communist and non-Communist nations.

Attributed to President Lyndon B. Johnson, the phrase "light at the end of the tunnel" became the signature quote of the Vietnam War during Johnson's administration. In November 1967 Johnson's advisers recommended that when discussing the war with the media, he should emphasize U.S. military progress. Initially, the strategy worked; Johnson's approval rating rose. However, American combat deaths rose significantly after the January 1968 Tet (New Year) Offensive in which the North Vietnamese army and the Vietcong attacked South Vietnamese cities. After Americans learned of the Tet Offensive, people used the phrase "light at the end of the tunnel" as a cynical joke. Johnson later remarked to his press secretary, Bill Moyers, "Light at the end of the tunnel? We don't even have a tunnel; we don't even know where the tunnel is!"

"Peace with Honor" was a phrase attributed to Richard Nixon, whose 1968 campaign promise was to withdraw American troops and end the war in Vietnam without sacrificing American honor or South

Vietnam. Marlette portrays this myth as a vulture carrying a laurel of peace. The contradiction portrayed in this image illustrates the inconsistency of Nixon's "Peace with Honor" plan. Early in Nixon's first term, many argued he betrayed promises of an honorable peace by the massive bombing of North Vietnam and the invasion of Cambodia. When criticized, Nixon defended his strategy, asking America to unite in seeking "not the peace of surrender, but peace with honor." Later, Nixon's critics maintained that the peace agreement negotiated in Paris was less than honorable because in secret negotiations with North Vietnam the United States betrayed South Vietnam. Nixon and his national security adviser, these analysts claim, knew South Vietnam would eventually fall to the Communists.

The last myth to be dispelled is the myth of the Communist bloodbath. Nixon had used fears of a Communist bloodbath in order to sustain the American anti-Communist effort in Vietnam. He said in a 1971 interview with the American Society of Newspaper Editors, "if the United States were to fail in Vietnam, if the Communists were to take over, the bloodbath that would follow would be a blot on this Nation's history from which we would find it very difficult to return." In fact, when North Vietnamese army forces occupied Saigon in 1975, the South Vietnamese government surrendered and the fighting ended. Although many South Vietnamese military and government personnel were incarcerated, no mass executions—no bloodbath—resulted.

About the Cartoonist

Doug Marlette was the cartoonist for the *Charlotte Observer* from 1972 to 1987, and the *Atlanta Constitution* from 1987 to 1989, where he won a Pulitzer Prize. He is also the creator of the comic strip *Kudzu*.

Examining Cartoon 5:
"What?... No Applause?!..."

About the Cartoon

In the cartoon Bob Gorrell criticizes President Bill Clinton's announcement on July 11, 1995, that his administration intended to normalize relations with Vietnam. Most of the opposition to this announcement came from veterans' groups and organizations representing prisoners of war (POWs) and the families of those missing in action (MIAs). These organizations believed that it was a betrayal to normalize relations with the Vietnamese government when it was withholding information on POWs and MIAs. At the end of the Vietnam War, 2,583 American prisoners were unaccounted for—missing or killed in action with no body recovered. The Communist postwar Vietnamese government demanded millions in "reparations" before it would assist in locating America's MIAs and known POWs. During the 1992 campaign, Clinton made a pledge to veterans' groups and POW/MIA families that he would demand the "fullest possible accounting" of their comrades and loved ones. Thus, when the administration announced it intended to normalize relations, these families felt betrayed. America's Vietnam veterans also felt let down because normalization meant consorting with the enemy against which they had sacrificed so much to fight. Gorrell portrays the disappointment of all these groups in the form of an armless, much-decorated Vietnam veteran who also represents America's POWs and MIAs. The cartoon suggests that Clinton should not be surprised he did not get any applause from these Americans for his efforts.

About the Cartoonist

Bob Gorrell's cartoons have appeared in newspapers and in magazines such as *Time, Newsweek, U.S. News & World Report, Business Week,* and *National Review.* He has also published an anthology, titled *Affairs of State,* and has won numerous awards.

Chronology

May 1941
Ho Chi Minh returns to Vietnam and establishes the League for Vietnamese Independence, also known as the Vietminh.

September 2, 1945
Ho Chi Minh declares Vietnamese independence, establishing the Democratic Republic of Vietnam.

November 23, 1946
French forces attack the Vietnamese harbor of Haiphong, beginning the first Vietnam war between France and the Vietminh.

July 26, 1950
President Truman authorizes $15 million in military aid to the French forces in Indochina.

September 30, 1953
President Dwight D. Eisenhower approves $785 million in military aid to support Vietnam against communism.

April 7, 1954
President Eisenhower explains his "domino theory" of foreign policy.

May 7, 1954
After the battle of Dien Bien Phu, French forces surrender to the Vietminh and begin withdrawing from Vietnam.

July 21, 1954
The Geneva Accords divide Vietnam along the 17th parallel, giving Ho Chi Minh's government control of North Vietnam and Bao Dai's government control of South Vietnam and requiring reunification

elections in 1956; Bao Dai denounces the agreement and the United States refuses to sign.

October 26, 1955
Ngo Dinh Diem defeats Bao Dai in the South Vietnamese election, establishes the Republic of Vietnam, and becomes the first president; Eisenhower pledges U.S. support.

July 20, 1956
The United States supports Diem's refusal to hold reunification elections.

May 1959
North Vietnam sends military personnel and weapons to support Communists in South Vietnam; the United States sends military advisers to South Vietnam.

December 1960
South Vietnamese rebels, called Vietcong (Vietnamese Communists) by Diem, form the National Liberation Front.

December 31, 1960
U.S. military personnel in Vietnam number nine hundred.

October 1961
President John F. Kennedy authorizes the deployment of more military advisers to South Vietnam and increases financial assistance to the Diem government.

December 31, 1961
U.S. military personnel in Vietnam number 3,205.

November 1, 1963
Diem is assassinated after a U.S.-supported military coup overthrows his government.

November 22, 1963
Kennedy is assassinated; Lyndon B. Johnson becomes president.

December 31, 1963
U.S. military personnel in Vietnam number 16,500.

August 2–4, 1964
The USS *Maddox*, an American destroyer, reports being attacked

by North Vietnamese patrol boats in the Gulf of Tonkin; the United States retaliates with air strikes on North Vietnam.

August 7, 1964
With only two dissenters, Congress passes the Gulf of Tonkin Resolution, giving Johnson authority to use "all necessary steps, including the use of armed force" in Southeast Asia.

December 31, 1964
U.S. military personnel in Vietnam number twenty-three thousand.

February 1965
North Vietnamese forces attack American bases in South Vietnam; Johnson authorizes Operation Rolling Thunder, a sustained bombing of North Vietnam that continues until October 31, 1968.

March 8, 1965
Thirty-five hundred U.S. Marines, the first U.S. combat troops, land in South Vietnam.

March 24, 1965
Antiwar teach-ins begin at American universities with the first teach-in at the University of Michigan at Ann Arbor.

April 7, 1965
Johnson offers a $1 billion economic development program for Vietnam if the North Vietnamese will participate in "unconditional discussion"; North Vietnamese prime minister Pham Van Dong rejects the proposal the next day.

April 17, 1965
Students for a Democratic Society sponsor the first major antiwar march in Washington, D.C.

October 15–16, 1965
Nationwide antiwar demonstrations begin.

December 31, 1965
U.S. military personnel in Vietnam number nearly 184,000.

January 28, 1966
Senator J. William Fulbright begins hearings of the Senate Foreign Relations Committee to investigate the Vietnam War.

December 31, 1966
U.S. military personnel in Vietnam number 385,000.

October 16–21, 1967
Antiwar demonstrations occur nationwide, including a march on the Pentagon in Washington, D.C.

December 31, 1967
U.S. military personnel in Vietnam number close to five hundred thousand.

January 30, 1968
Communist forces launch the Tet Offensive, a massive surprise attack on South Vietnamese cities during the Vietnamese New Year, which U.S. and South Vietnamese forces repulse after nearly a month of fighting.

March 16, 1968
In South Vietnam, Lieutenant William Calley orders his men to fire on the village of My Lai, killing hundreds of unarmed civilians.

March 31, 1968
Johnson suspends the bombing of North Vietnam, invites peace talks with North Vietnam, and announces that he will not run for reelection.

May 13, 1968
The United States and North Vietnam begin peace talks in Paris, France.

October 31, 1968
Johnson halts the bombing of North Vietnam, ending Operation Rolling Thunder.

December 31, 1968
U.S. military personnel in Vietnam number 540,000.

June 8, 1969
President Richard Nixon announces the first withdrawal of twenty-five thousand U.S. troops from Vietnam; U.S. military personnel in Vietnam number 543,000.

October 15, 1969
More than 1 million Americans participate in the moratorium antiwar demonstrations nationwide.

November 3, 1969

Nixon requests the support of the "silent majority" for his Vietnamization plan to gradually withdraw U.S. troops from Vietnam while shifting military responsibilities to South Vietnamese forces.

November 15, 1969

The mobilization peace demonstration in Washington, D.C., draws 250,000 people, becoming the largest antiwar protest in U.S. history.

December 31, 1969

U.S. military personnel in Vietnam number 479,000.

February 20, 1970

National Security Adviser Henry Kissinger begins secret peace talks with North Vietnamese negotiator Le Duc Tho in Paris.

April 29, 1970

U.S. and South Vietnamese forces invade Cambodia to attack Communist sanctuaries; major antiwar protests start nationwide.

May 4, 1970

Ohio National Guardsmen kill four antiwar protesters at Kent State University.

June 24, 1970

The U.S. Senate repeals the 1964 Gulf of Tonkin Resolution; U.S. troops withdraw from Cambodia.

December 31, 1970

U.S. military personnel in Vietnam number 335,000.

March 29, 1971

A military court convicts Lieutenant William Calley of murdering South Vietnamese civilians at My Lai.

April 19–23, 1971

The group Vietnam Veterans Against the War demonstrates in Washington, D.C.

June 13, 1971

The *New York Times* begins publication of the Pentagon Papers, secret defense documents stolen by Daniel Ellsberg.

December 31, 1971
U.S. military personnel in Vietnam number close to 150,000.

March 1972
Communist forces begin the Easter Offensive against South Vietnam.

May 8, 1972
Nixon authorizes the mining of Haiphong Harbor, a naval blockade of North Vietnam, and intensified bombing of North Vietnam.

October 1972
Kissinger and Le Duc Tho reach a cease-fire agreement.

December 1972
When peace talks break down, Nixon orders the resumption of the bombing of North Vietnam.

December 31, 1972
U.S. military personnel in Vietnam number twenty-four thousand.

January 27, 1973
The Paris Peace Accords are signed, ending U.S. involvement in the Vietnam War.

March 29, 1973
North Vietnam releases the final sixty-seven American prisoners of war and the last U.S. troops leave Vietnam.

December 31, 1973
U.S. military personnel in Vietnam number less than 250.

September 1974
President Gerald Ford pardons Nixon for any crimes he might have committed as president and offers clemency to draft evaders and military deserters.

April 30, 1975
South Vietnam falls to the North Vietnamese as the last Americans leave by helicopter from the roof of the U.S. embassy.

January 21, 1977
President Jimmy Carter pardons most of the ten thousand Vietnam War draft evaders on the day after his inauguration.

December 1978

Vietnam invades Cambodia in response to the 1977 Cambodian incursion into Vietnam; thousands of "boat people" flee Vietnam after Vietnamese efforts to nationalize industries and collectivize farms create food shortages.

February 17, 1979

China attacks Vietnam to protest Vietnam's invasion of Cambodia but withdraws sixteen days later.

November 11, 1982

The Vietnam Veterans Memorial, known as "the Wall," is dedicated in Washington, D.C.

April 30, 1990

Vietnamese Communist Party leader Nguyen Van Linh appeals to the United States for friendship and economic cooperation.

April 21, 1991

The United States and Vietnam agree to establish a U.S. office in Hanoi to help determine the fate of all soldiers missing in action.

July 11, 1995

With bipartisan support in Congress, President Bill Clinton announces the normalization of relations with Vietnam.

November 16, 2000

Clinton visits Vietnam.

October 3, 2001

The U.S. Senate approves an agreement normalizing trade between the United States and Vietnam.

For Further Research

Books

David L. Anderson, ed., *Shadow on the White House: Presidents and the Vietnam War, 1945–1975*. Lawrence: University Press of Kansas, 1993.

James R. Arnold, *The First Domino: Eisenhower, the Military, and America's Intervention in Vietnam*. New York: William Morrow, 1991.

Larry Berman, *No Peace, No Honor: Nixon, Kissinger, and Betrayal in Vietnam*. New York: Free Press, 2001.

Charles DeBenedetti, *An American Ordeal: The Antiwar Movement of the Vietnam Era*. Syracuse, NY: Syracuse University Press, 1990.

Gerard J. DeGroot, *A Noble Cause? America and the Vietnam War*. New York: Longman, 2000.

Gilbert N. Dorland, *Legacy of Discord: Voices of the Vietnam War*. Washington, DC: Brassey's, 2001.

Lloyd C. Gardner, *Pay Any Price: Lyndon Johnson and the Wars for Vietnam*. Chicago: Ivan R. Dee, 1995.

George C. Herring, *America's Longest War: The United States and Vietnam, 1950–1975*. New York: John Wiley, 1979.

David E. Kaiser, *American Tragedy: Kennedy, Johnson, and the Origins of the Vietnam War*. Cambridge, MA: Harvard University Press, 2000.

Stanley Karnow, *Vietnam: A History*. New York: Penguin, 1991.

Fredrik Logevall, *The Origins of the Vietnam War*. New York: Longman, 2001.

Robert Mann, *A Grand Delusion: America's Descent into Vietnam*. New York: Basic Books, 2001.

Orrin Schwab, *Defending the Free World: John F. Kennedy, Lyndon Johnson, and the Vietnam War, 1961–1965*. Westport, CT: Praeger, 1998.

Ezra Y. Siff, *Why the Senate Slept: The Gulf of Tonkin Resolution and the Beginning of America's Vietnam War*. Westport, CT: Praeger, 1999.

Tom Wells, *The War Within: America's Battle over Vietnam*. Berkeley: University of California Press, 1994.

Political Cartoon Books

Tony Auth, *Behind the Lines*. Boston: Houghton Mifflin, 1977.

Herbert Block, *Herblock on All Fronts*. New York: New American Library, 1980.

———, *Herblock Special Report*. New York: Norton, 1974.

———, *Herblock's State of the Union*. New York: Simon and Schuster, 1972.

Paul Conrad, *Drawn & Quartered*. New York: Harry N. Abrams, 1985.

———, *Pro and Conrad*. San Rafael, CA: Neff-Kane, 1979.

Jules Feiffer, *Feiffer on Nixon: The Cartoon Presidency*. New York: Random House, 1974.

Foreign Policy Association, eds., *A Cartoon History of United States Foreign Policy*. New York, Random House, 1967.

———, eds., *1776–1976: A Cartoon History of United States Foreign Policy*. New York: William Morrow, 1975.

Steven Heller, ed., *Jules Feiffer's America: From Eisenhower to Reagan.* New York: Alfred A. Knopf, 1982.

Nancy King and Foreign Policy Association, eds., *A Cartoon History of United States Foreign Policy: From 1945 to the Present.* New York: Pharos Books, 1991.

Ranan R. Lurie, *Nixon-Rated Cartoons.* New York: Quadrangle, 1974.

G.B. Trudeau, *Doonesbury's Greatest Hits.* New York: Holt, Rinehart and Winston, 1978.

Don Wright, *Wright On.* New York: Simon and Schuster, 1971.

Web Sites

The American Experience: Vietnam Online, www.pbs.org/wgbh/amex/vietnam. Vietnam Online was developed to accompany *Vietnam: A Television History*, a television series produced by WGBH Boston. The Web site contains transcripts of the programs, a time line, biographies of key personalities, a bibliography of personal reflections, and links to maps, bibliographies, and other Web sites.

Recalling the Vietnam War, http://globetrotter.berkeley.edu/PubEd/research/vietnam.html. On this Web site sixteen people, some of whom played a role in Vietnam War policy, provide commentary on the causes and consequences of U.S. decisions in Vietnam. Included are political activist Noam Chomsky, strategic analyst Daniel Ellsberg, and former secretary of defense Robert McNamara.

Index

Americans
   on fall of Saigon, 57–58
   impact of Pentagon Papers on
      opinion of, 8
   mistrust of Johnson by, 26–27
   requesting aid for South Viet-
      nam from, 55–56
   on South Vietnamese refugees,
      60
   watching war on television and,
      7–8
   see also antiwar movement
Americans for Democratic Action,
   11
antiwar movement, 30–31, 32–33
   invasion of Cambodia and, 38
   mainstream Americans and,
      11–12
   at the 1968 Democratic
      National Convention, 10–11
   Nixon's peace plan and, 37–38
   students and, 8–9
   Vietnam veterans and, 9–10
Army of the Republic of
   Vietnam, 23, 37, 38

Ball, George, 26
Baltimore Sun (newspaper), 35
Bellocq, Pierre, 28–29
Block, Herbert, 47, 59–61

Buddhists, 19, 23
Bush, George H.W., 15
Bush, George W., 15

Calley, William, 9
Cambodia, 37–38, 41
cartoons
   on arguments justifying U.S.
      intervention, 62–64
   on bombing of North Vietnam,
      44–45
   on Clinton normalizing
      relations with Vietnam,
      65–66
   on draft lottery, 42–43
   on fall of Saigon, 57–58
   on Ford requesting aid for
      South Vietnam, 55–56
   on government spending under
      Johnson, 34–35
   on Johnson administration's
      policy on communism, 28–29
   on Johnson's military strategies,
      30–31
   on Kennedy's role in Diem's
      fall, 23
   on Nixon's Vietnamization plan,
      40–41, 48–49
   on resolution of Kent State
      shootings, 46–47

South Vietnam, 19
  Ford requesting aid for, 55–56
  refugees in U.S. from, 59–60
  suffering of people from, 60–61
Soviet Union, 62
  Communist threat and, 18, 63
  reasons for U.S. intervention
    and, 52
Stalin, Joseph, 18
St. Louis Post-Dispatch (newspaper),
  31
Students for a Democratic Society
  (SDS), 9
suicide, 6, 56

Teamsters, the, 11
television, 7–8
Tet Offensive, 8, 27
Thieu, Nguyen Van, 37, 39, 49
Trudeau, Garry, 57–58
Truman, Harry S., 17, 52
Truman Doctrine, 18
Twenty-Sixth Amendment, 14

Uncle Sam, 20, 21
United Auto Workers (UAW), 11
United States
  as cause of conflict in Vietnam,
    53
  Geneva Accords and, 18–19
  intervention in Vietnam, 20, 22,
    62–64
  arguments against, 53–54
  early, 17–18
  reasons for, 51–53
  Vietnamese people suffering
    from, 60–61
  South Vietnamese refugees in,
    59–60

University of Michigan, 9
U.S. News & World Report
  (magazine), 49

Valtman, Edmund S., 32–33
veterans
  difficulties faced by, 6–7, 56
  disabled, 6
  opposing normalization of
    relations with Vietnam,
    65–66
  opposition to war by, 9–10
  suicide by, 6, 56
Vietcong, 19
  body counts and, 26
Vietminh, 18, 21
Vietnam
  Geneva Accords and, 18–19
  independence movement in,
    17–18
  normalizing relations with,
    65–66
  see also South Vietnam
Vietnam Moratorium Committee
  (VMC), 11
Vietnam Syndrome, 15
Vietnam War
  legacy of, 14–15
  moratoriam on, 11–12
voting age, 14

Washington, D.C., march (1965),
  9
Westmoreland, William C., 54
Winter Soldier Investigation,
  9
Wright, Don, 43

Yardley, Richard, 35